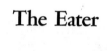

The Eater

Also by Peter Michelson:
The Aesthetics of Pornography

The Eater

Peter Michelson

THE SWALLOW PRESS INC.

CHICAGO

Published by
The Swallow Press Incorporated
1139 South Wabash Avenue
Chicago, Illinois 60605

This book is printed on 100% recycled paper

ISBN (cloth) 0-8040-0593-1
ISBN (paper) 0-8040-0594-X
LIBRARY OF CONGRESS CATALOG CARD NUMBER 78-189187

New Poetry Series No. 45

Some of these poems have appeared in the following magazines
and anthologies: *Chicago Review, Tri-Quarterly, North American
Review, Beanfest I, Choice, Mojo Navigator(e), New Orleans
Review, The Prairie Schooner, The Young American Writers,
New Poetry Anthology I.* Others of these poems have minded
their own business.

for Eugene Wildman, John Matthias, and Michael Anania

A man (he thinks *poet*) has friends and he is in luck. They tell him what he wants to hear. And, when he is most in luck, what he does not want to hear: there is work to be done. "Because basically I am an inarticulate man." Someday, someday I will say it right. If my luck holds. Either then, or never. Will the sun rise tomorrow? Yes.

contents

advertisement

Reader, my guess is . . .
you needs a whetting to your tastes
not to mention a wondering
to your pander. You're

standing by the pomeshelf
in one—no more than two—of the twenty bookstores that
sells poems across this great

land (Reader, I want it understood here and now that
rumours about my competitors notwithstanding—those
nameless and incompetent
assholes—I
like, nay *love*, my country: I
have never gone back where I came from, much
to my poor, overburdened mother's
relief; I, even tho the
army scorned me, never
burned my draft card; and
twice when I was in trouble I
called the cops rather than a hippy—though
I did once ask one for a match, *which
he did not have*, showing
what you can expect from them!) and

you wonders should you buy a book by
Gary Snyder or Don Lee or Lawrence Ferlinghetti! Don't
do it, Reader. They are freaks.

To a man they love *other things*
more than their country! More
than their mother! And

don't buy that book of Immortal Poems of the English
Language. It
is filled with Beauty, Reader. The opiate of the rich.

Buy this very book you
are holding in your hands. Patronize
us Reader, we
are a small and dwindling group who

love our mothers, who
love our country, who
despise drugs, who don't, like decadent
Salomes, want things handed to us on a platter.

Don't drive us to freakerie, Reader.
Buy this book.

The pains, Reader, the pains we have taken
to make a pure American product. This
book was printed in Indiana,
Indiana, Reader, the

heart of the country.
In a union shop.
For a union wage.
Printed, for your protection,
by American printers, who will not
print lies, slander or filth. Not

in Europe or Japan, like
some of your publishers, where
taste and labor is cheap and
the dollar is drained. Moreover,

the price is right, Reader,
a fair price for
good American-made merchandise. A

x

reasonable margin of prifit for the publisher, Reader,
you can understand that,
    he's a business man,
    it's the American way.

        And Reader I promise,
        cross my heart and hope to die,
that whatever money I make I will spend right here

            in the good old U.S. of A. For
mortgages, cars, color televisions, credit cards, and interest.

Not, like a lot of your poets,
        fritter it away
galavanting around the world
    badmouthing the fatherland.

        There are no foreign words here, Reader,
not one! I
        don't even *know* any foreign words.

    Try it, Reader, you'll *like* it.

        The writing in this book is
"bawdy, wildly funny, and sometimes serious and direct."
            That's a *quote*, Reader,
            not some huckster or
    fancy intellectual snob critic, but

            a quote in a country newspaper
    in plain American
by an ordinary salt-of-the-earth citizen like yourself.

        Wildly funny, Reader,
            sometimes serious and direct.

Oh Reader
        I hear America singing.

True, a little bawdry
but we Americans know about that
don't we Reader,
a little spice but
basically good clean fun.

Man to man stuff, Reader,
not for your sissy queers
and romantics, man
to man, for red-blooded Americans,
in the locker room,
behind the barn.

Reader, we're Americans together.
I know you. You know me.
We understand each other.
You'll eat the eyes out of this book!

Consume it
with a friend, Reader, with your wife, your husband—eat
chew eat chew eat chew, he
reads that, you read Oh
how I'd like to, it
makes me feel soooo good to
and you me tooo

be sure you read it
out loud, together
at home around the fire, a
family book

eatcheweatcheweatchew(Oh
how I'd like to)eatcheweatcheweatchew(it
makes me feel so good to)eatcheweatcheweatchew(and
you me tooo)eatcheweatcheweatchew. . . . .

Get it, Reader?
Wild fun?!
Don't you feel *good*?

When you ask,
what does it all mean,
must the poet always answer
less and less?!

No, No, Reader, a thousand times NO.

It's high time we accentuate the positive, the
good things in this great land of ours—Oh
Reader, Reader,
what more can I say . . . . What More . . . .

Please, Please, Reader
BUY AMERICAN!

Notary Sojac, Reader, from
The Eater
P.S. (This
preface is plain
ly pandering but
what's inside ain't
so easy.
You guts got the
money
?

I

in my craw, miscellaneously

the eater
(a fat man's lullaby)

"Euclid alone has looked on Beauty bare."
—Edna St. Vicent Millay

Euclid be damned
God damn his eunuch forms
I require shape for consummation, bare:
fruits have it
apples
in their erotic skins
but plums too and pears
and even dates
incite my flare
for appetite

The business of the eater
    is to eat,
be opulent in ruminating
    flesh and pulp:
Let his organs operate
    at will—
a split sphincter is
an affirmation still:

Let tooth and tongue go
    bare, dredging juice and rind—
Yesss this world's succulent:
    Tooth! Tongue!
Forth upon the firmament!
    Eating to and fro in it,
melons roundly ripe and fair,
    hot meat wet and rare—
Lip lascivious, soft you Tongue, reverently
    and Tooth you most lustfully must ravage!

3

Fair's fair, plump's plump,
but fat's the better thing—
It is this eater's gorge(ousness),
his gluttony, I sing

The eater prospers so
to eat and eats to
prosper fatly
Let him who will
go sveltly cloaked and trim,

the eater must pursue
    his plan;
assault the symmetries of shape—
        the shapely grapes
        incline to sin,
        and a withered one,
        however chaste,
        is after all
        a flaccid skin
so the eater must
    pursue his plan
assaulting shape
    as best he can

The business of the eater is
    to consummate
The business of the eater is
    to generate

The eater has prodigious plans
Ahh, yes, the eater is a lovely man.

what the eater teaches

I too
an apostle, my
creed I do
not **BELIEVE**—but
share the wealth I
say: I'm a teacher
and a **MORALIST!** a man
who pays his debts, more or
less. So I shall (i.e.
according to my ability)
give angels
CARNAL
knowledge!
APOCALYPTIC
CONTRADICTIONS:
PENETRABILITY
I say: objects
occupying the same
space at
the same time: having
connections, associations, and
RELATIONS
(leave ideas to
your betters!) con-
ti-gu-i-ty's the thing,
and **VISIONS**—be-
fore me I see delerious
DAISY CHAINS
of cherub and
seraphim giggling
CAVORTING
passing in their lively
fingertips outrageous
PALPS

5

of **TOUCHTOUCHTOUCH**, make
beasts of many shapes and
sizes. . . . All
this I teach, at
no **RISK** of
profit or **PLEASURE** to myself.

going hungry at our lady's place

At Notre Dame
today is
the Feast of the Absorption—
All work stops—

Though brazen Moses'
angry toes grip and
finger prick the
muddled sky,

Though infidel riveters—or
believers
moonlighting—
hammer home our
lady's newest sporting
house,

Though prophecy and
sporting life
make hay, the

library—its
gold and quartzite Christ
upstaging Cecil B.
DeMille—is
dark beneath that
slab faced
blessing.

I want books

and curse the dark
beneath Christ's brow—my
calendar toasts
only
famine—What
now?

7

Before me, Moses
glowering Christ's love, behind,
            the riveting's unholy
        clatter—with
            business so abruptly

            altered
        my day's coherence is
    displaced—idled and irreverent, I
                            am much
                ungraced.

definition from hunger

Nigger, pig, commie, kike, and
whore are all in genus bogey—a
noun derived from Scot. *bogle,*
meaning spectre, itself
derived from M.E. *bugger,* meaning
what it will, or
M.E. *bugge,* meaning bug, or
A.S. *bungle,* meaning
bungle: hence, legally and socially, a
mistake of God to be fucked perversely
or squashed.

It's cold, a ragged Chicago wind off the lake, and—after drinks at Ricardo's where we went to see the mad Ivan Albright painting behind the circle bar because an artist friend told me to—Susan's coat is too slight. So, for no reason, not knowing her well enough even to know if she would smoke it, I light a cigar for her, and go off to get the car, leaving her with the black doorman and Mexican hatcheck lady and the cigar. When I get back, the doorman has asked her why she is smoking the cigar. Why not, she says. He laughs. So does the hatcheck lady. So does Susan. Her smoking the cigar makes them all, in that moment, happy. They will never be unhappy in that moment. The doorman is so pleased he forgets to do his job. Susan opens the door for herself, still laughing and puffing the cigar. She brings some of the happiness into the car.

from bonwit teller

In the happy Halloween of
            Christmas, when
                        fake graybeard
                                    fatstuffs clang
            charity abroad, walk the
            lighted boulevard's fantastic
    inundation, find

some gift,
            give,
                        ride the holy season
            gladden the heart
                        of some executive, join
            the masque of buyer
    and seller, come
            in from the boulevard,
                        come in, to Bonwit Teller—

            come in, come up
                to the mezzanine
                                do
                        your shopping at
                Club Eight-Nineteen. Be-
                        hind that door,
                                    leering Chinese
                        Red, your
                visions await you   as

        the model Noreen—

    lavishly lacquered, neckline
precise,
            Noreen will greet you
                        profuse in the service she
                                sells, subtle

10

at arts of *un*
and *re*
dress—

Noreen, you take
my coat with
such an easy aire, you
serve my gin with
a Geisha's studied care—
Noreen, I
browse and warm
to your conversation, your
shoulder's con-
figuration distracting but
discretely
bare—

Noreen, you model
your filigree peek-a-boo
slip, moulded
for breeding
extravagant richly of hip—Noreen
you exquisite
untouchable
whore

your
merchandise wastes
in that department store.

the eater goes 1) west, or 2) to the movies

Here sand throbs and
                cactus pricks
            the flaccid air. In
                such glare beside
        this burning stone a
    diamond-back rasps and
            coils just where
                I'd walk. In

    the movies   Randolph
                Scott rides up   hard
    lipped   and   drills   long   muscley
            (broad grins grinned
        here) drills ol' snake,
                    reins up
                    hard,
                swinging long

        levied   (Mr. Scott's
            wardrobe by Levi Straus, the
    man who won/dressed the west) I say he
                        swings long levied leg over
            puckered buckskin haunch pivoting
        in stirrup and
                holsters steeley   *long* (grin)
    ol' Colt .45 before
                he hits ground im-
                    pressive in dust
                    cloud
        touching thumb and trigger

            finger, to brim and
                smiles *howdy ma'am* stretch-

                            12

ing lips across his
        froooty white teeth, tight
        sphincter emitting no
sign of exertion from
    man or beast (fan-
            tastic so cooool), while
I (ooh sin, shame, and degra-
        dation) I
            present my parts (blush).   Her
    parts are blushing says lab
            technician making no-
            tation and adjusting elect-
            rodes.   Her parts, he
            muses, blushing hmmmmmmmm
        But

    Here / Now / Among
        these waiting sands   I
            suck in and
        loathe this air
            face this
                snake a-
    lone,   much too afraid to
            fight too paralyzed for
                flight—hang
        dog to know that should
    I ride I'd be
    obliged to sit
    astride—so . . . . say:
is him a hairy or a slick palmed her-
        maphroditic Grace reclined awhile
            beguiled at
            that cocked snake and
        me ungunned, face
        to mortal face?

13

fragment from fargo #2
(for cap't. ahab)

In the window
of a store
in Fargo
North Dakota
a too fat fish
in a too flat puddle
splashes its pudgy body
wedging between the waves
and the littler fish.
They flit away.
Confusion in the pool.
In the glass,
my image grinning
out as
I am grinning in.

whatever happened to rita hayworth

was that she said to Jack Lemmon   then
                                  a punk kid

      trapped
by a fallen steel girder
           in the basement of   the U.S.S. Heart

          of Darkness, where
         he keeps stroking his beard and saying,
"This too has been one of the dark places of the earth,"

         until Joseph P. Levine Presents,
the producer, goes apeshit   shrieking
    "Punk,
shave that fucking beard,"   and kicks
        a steel girder which, this being
               Hollywood, collapses on the kid

        which is how
           he got stuck there
in the aftermath of a sinking ship in the first place,
         when Rita

                  Hayworth sashays (that
           is to say she threw all her pounds from
        the hips on down, alternating
                      hips, because
it ain't watcha got it's whatcha do with whatcha got, which is the

        story of how
Rita Hayworth survived—or did
        she?—into the age of Brigitte

               Bardot), howsoever
that may be she sashays up (zoom front, crotch/pan back, ass) to

the kid, pinned
and wriggling, up to his
anal apperature in rising bilge but still
Marlovian:

"And this too has been one of the dark places of the earth,"

he says, not
unmindful that Zukini or
Buggeratti or Fellatio or some other arty Wop
might wander into the Roman Cinema after a sportive night
with
decadent aristocrats ("plays Bach like that,
and shot hisself!"   "Couldn't make
C sharp on his organ."   "Pretty fucking tragic,

that's what!") and ogling
huge inscrutable one-eyed flounders like they do

and discover
the Lemmon to star in a far-out   Itralian
version of "When Moses
Saw God's Hinder Parts, or The Sweet Smell of Success," but

Miss Hayworth does
her job the best she can,   and
takes to licking his
palm (suggestively!) between the

index and foreplay fingers across his life line to
the wrist where she lays a couple
lascivious swirls on his pulse,   saying

"Are you sure you can't get free tonight?"

whereupon
the kid, aspiring al-
ways to high art, thinks he is in Martial's

16

mac Lure play and
      says, "Fanfuckintastic!   I
           think I can erect
          an excuse." Which he does, saying,
        "I thought I could," and, easily disengaging

        himself from the
      girder, he figures from there
      on it's all downhill,   only
          to hear Rita say, as

  he approaches her with
palpitating eyes,   *"You don't want me!* (which,
         strictly speaking, was not true but
       was all right to say for the purposes of
         the picture which after all, rather than
     Miss Hayworth, is what the kid was supposed
        to be making,
      showing that Hollywood knows about
         art, contrary to appearances, when
    it can have Rita Hayworth tell such a
     beautiful though obvious lie, not
       to mention not mixing business with
     pleasure which the ugly rumor
     about it is)

You don't want me! (she says)/*Armies* have marched over me!"

Now *this*, strictly speaking, *was* true,
      though it is not clear
      from the celluloid
         nature of the statement whether   she

               meant those of Ghengis
                 Khan's cousin

   Alley Oop Khan, whose armies
then as now were the scourge of the far west and

17

who was so named because even though
he was from Caldwell, Idaho

he could
jump very high and
thus himself became the Black Scourge

of the Czar's key stadium at
catching passes—many of which were disgracefully

thrown
at Miss Hayworth (a better than average
receiver), though some, this being the home of

the Mattachine Society, were
also thrown at Hustling Hugh McElhenny (a less
than average receiver), misnamed by a hopeful gay publicity

agent for the 69ers but
since traded for Peter Orlovsky, Allen
Gingsberg, and two
future neophyte monks (all considered

good receivers) to Gary
Snyder's Kyoto Bearcats, where, known as
The Voice of the Pink Peril, Hustling Hugh annouces

the Bearcats slashing
meditational style of play in the zen manner, for
instance—"October afternoon, a
certain slant / off
tackle, line/
past, Ah
light."

Or whether she meant
the armies of Frankie Sinatra which
then as now occupied Chicago and Lake Tahoe, because

                    Miss Hayworth
          occasionally had delusions
      of grandeur and thought she was Ava Gardner,   under which

                                misinformation she
            once married a Mexican matador, only to be
deserted
when he moved up to Barcelona

              in the Three-I
          League, at which point she   thought she was

                    Marilyn Monroe and
      married an outfielder, who it turned out was good hit no
          field (or, as crazy
          Leonard used to chant—"Who
                can run and hit and throw / Better
                  than his brother Joe? / Why,
                    it's Dominic Dimaggio!), so

              still looking for
      a real passer, and by this time   supposing she was
                                Jane Russell, she married
                a quarter back, a tough cookie but much given to
          passing water   which was not
                    one of her things, so for no
      clear reason whatsoever she decided she was Leontyne Price

              and married (much
      to everyone's distress) an Italian tenor,   alas

                          a vestigial castrati,
      and, since one Italian tenor is very like another, things
          seemed to be

                    going in circles, so
          her agent put her out to stud, announcing
                                that
                      the whole thing had got
              out of control.   But,

                        19

inasmuch as she
moved around to a lot of studios   scholars have to this day

been ignorant of
which army she meant—Frankie's or
Aly's (as Miss Hayworth affectionately called him
in happier days), or whether she might not have meant, inscrut-

ably, Audrey Hepburn's
in 'War and Peace" or Pamela Mason's army of women's liberation
in "The Desert Fox" or

perhaps even
Bogart's dried up little one in "Sahara."   There

is much dispute. Lately
the whole thing has been turned over to J. Edgar Hoover, who

with full federal support
has been taking plaster foot casts from the

parade grounds
of *all* armies on earth, real and imagined, and
comparing them with the individual footprints of
all the *people*
on earth, real and imagined, to
be used as evidence when the time comes.   These

plaster footprints,
along with the pornography he confiscated from

Copenhagen (as
being a threat to the defense perimeter of America)

and a complete recording
of all telephone conversations in the world

for the past twenty-five

years, he is storing in King Farouk's tomb, which
              by order of Spiro Agnew   the Israeli's

                              appropriated from Egypt
              as not only a center of filth, decadence, and unchristian

                          behavior, but
              also as an undeniable gathering place of Egyptian nationals

                              which not even
                  the Russians denied. And that
              by and large is whatever happened to Rita Hayworth.

getting hustled in a laramie bar

Fantastic!
Laramie! Gay?
Blows (so to speak) my mind,   in

the face of all
this sullen, uptight cowboy
virility.   Must

be from
Chicago, New York, L.A..
No,   says he's from Big Piney, Wyoming.

A curly headed, burly
buttocked student at
the university of Wyoming, home
of the Cowboys.   Plump enough to play football.

Why me?
(Discrete Art Models, Inc.
present Pete—fat, bald, white, 33, straight,
indifferently hung, no interest in leather or discipline—
now travelling in the west;

Come on guys, get
this one while he's in your town!)   Fucking
faggot's got no taste.   Steps

up to the bar
just like a real
person, catches my eye:

"Hi," he says,
"you at the university?"   Then some bullshit
from me about teaching, etc.

which he is obviously
not

interested in.   Then
     more bullshit from me   about   what does *he* do
                    (student, secondary edu-
               cation, graduating, going—where
          else?—to San Franciso) which he is also

                    not interested in.
          "You (i.e. me) live around here?" "Live by
               yourself?" (moves over two barstools
                    next to me and starts vaguely
                    subtle game of kneesies)

          "Get lonely, living
     alone?" Shit, there must be some Explorer
          Scout Handbook for queers that
                    gives a standard
                         routine.

                         But the kid
               can't   quite   figure me out: AC or DC?

                    Finally,
          "You straight?" I confess.
     "Sorry about that." I give him my best
                         well-what-the-fuck-forget-it shrug.

          "Let's keep it between
     us."   Cosmopolitan assurance   from me.   He

                              waits a decent interval,
               about 7 seconds, and, as I'm
          about to say something insane   like how
does a cute little dyke like you   make it   in a town like this,

               he splits, off to
          shake his burly buttocks in a

frug or twist or something with a college
chick.   Does she, japing her
ass around the

floor, know he prefers me
to it?   How about that   cowboy, does he?

No.   It's between us.   Him,
jabbing his well zipped dick at the chick (maybe, being

a native mountain man, he makes it
with everything—bears and coyotes, too), and

me, watching my only chance
in Laramie for (literally) a piece of ass   jerk on
with his second choice.

Oh well, things are looking up.
Shit, a place that breeds indigenous queers can't be all bad.

the massage, or, do
not celebrate the fourth of july

The massage
is an extension of irregularity: ir-

regularity
is an extension of
regularity:

Ex-Lax is
an extension of anality, and

therefore
it follows that
defecation is an extention of mastication, as

is (easily)
the bedpan of the toilet: thus

as the mountain is an extension
of the dunghill, so

is Mohammad of
the mobile mind of the creator:
similarly,

the bowels being an extension of man,
and man an extension of God,
it will be seen (if
only by Moishe) that

the sphincter is an extension of the holy hinder parts,

from which we may conclude that

25

      (in Judeo-Christian cultures)
plumbing is an extention of revelation, or

                        (in classical cultures) that
            the toilet is an extension of posterior analytics:

        there is, in short,
    absolutely no inevitability,   *if*

                        you are willing to contemplate
                    what is happening (?)

            pull the chain (!)
                            contemplate

                the glass bottomed toilet
                bowl test tube pipes LePage's
                    Transparant Glue (miss nothing)

    follow   that turd
                to its logical conclusion:

                shit knows no country, the
        suspicious bowels of cosmonauts, the
                delicious bowels of astronauts   contribute

                        (each in their own heart, each
                in their own way) to

        our excremental atmosphere:
                        offal-in-orbit is, then,
                an extension of the sewer,   and

            the sewer being an extension of the cesspool, the
    cosmos is an extension of the septic tank:

                    we are all in up to our lower lip!
                        (pity the little children!) this

is total emergency: do
        not, I repeat, *do not*
               celebrate the Fourth of July,

      even lady fingers make waves.

II

i too, alone in the dark

after a mural
(for donna)

The woman holds perhaps a wren.
Two children watch the bird their mother holds.
The bird commands the scene.

Suppose the hands to stiffen,
drop the startled bird,
the children's eyes expanding in surprise,
the bird's terrific strain to fly, its eyes
and wings agape,   its floundering absurd—
suppose that it should fly,
recover ballast, straighten on the wing
and sweep beyond the scene into some sky,
scuttling poise to ride the wind and sing . . .

But now the bird commands this tranquil scene—
Cradled with the dignity it knows,
it is suspended by the grace a queen
or saint would grant a portrait in tableau:
The bird is held—that makes the piece serene.

vines from the eater's
stalk, or it's 4 a.m.
my darling daughters

Arms Chaplinesque
legs akimbo
you mime
your frantic semaphores
and bawl
until
I play the wetnurse
to your thirst.

Outrageous
in presumption
your miasmic prepossession
fumbles any adjacent thing
to be its teat,
so
you suck
my knuckle for a treat.

Discontent
to gum
my unrewarding fist
you shriek
commands,
break wind
upon the world's head,

and so direct
the force of things
to fill your belly
that I'm coerced,
in fact

concede,
as you conspire
with what
delicate
greed.

the eater looks back

You were
the more deceived, it seemed, you

wanted Love, Romance   you Heloise.

And while we   professed devotion   and
you defined our
happy zodiac of mind,   I

plotted with my palms to
stroke your nobler soul,   my goal
your contour's concupiscent
promotion.

But even there,   in our massive eloquence
of passion, your
prevailing reason contrived

its best.   My
wonder now is how—when
my rancid brain was broiling for
your moonlit breast, when
my pubescent body, though feathered
something like a dove, mangled
grace to drench you in nectars of my
lust—how you turned
that naked hankering to *Love*.

I did my damndest
to make our fleshes
sullied,   but

your dialectic, unlike your
better part, was
beyond my penetration—you

turned my fine demonic thrust
to *adoration.*   Our
                craving bodies mating
                molded as
        they couldn't help but do,   and

                even this you airily
                        construed . . . our parts
                you said were jointly made and
        'honored with the ambrosian stamp of Aphrodites' seal.'

                        God
                I marveled at your mighty
                        craving for the True and
        elaborate ignoring of the real.

            Now, years later, I
        still evade your awful oversoul, and

                        like Keats' Greeks my
                life consists
                        in ever winning near
                but never quite the goal.

                And for our separate labors

            I've
        become a father
        and you a mother.   Though

                for years we've not been lovers, or
                        even neighbors, I
                        keep looking back

                to find
        the young and breathy shudder that

                        you, far wiser,
                        knew to be the dying aphrodisiac.

hungry eye at the flin flon
(union pier, michigan)

Drummer, band, raucous roadhouse
rhythms—girls coiffured, manicured, petite
teenage chic, jeans. Boys
indisputably Aryan,
clean. Hausfraus—bland and
sagging—hoard their beer, wait glumly
for foxtrots, each other.
Schlitz flicks asteroids through
the dark, Hamm's glows eternal
Gitchee Gumee, and at the bar
the baptized hunch and over-
hang their stools.   GENTS and LADIES
glowing brutal orange diffuse
democratic auras of latrine . . .

From this you
rise and dance Diana,
Aphrodite—your

torso contours Bacchic
graces, such bones / such flesh transform

these mortal places, you
dance, smile and Cleopatra's walk

you mimic, laughing, mock
this myth, my need: your
magnitude of leg, of
hip, hair, and shoulder prove

a goddess once was real, you
bring a bronze to life, a
vision richer, older—your

                    sweeping poniard
                         fingers rake my
strings—ragged down below, above my demon sings

                              erotic
                    at the swirl your hair
             in gloried orange and bluelit brings. . . . Your

        sandaled instep arcs   and
             flexing
        rams my eye a rivet hotly

                    up your seam . . .
             eyes like molten dreams
        along your Levi seams find your

                    shadowed secret tautly
                         molded spots: that
             moving marbles me, but
        motion moves a motion if even only air—your

                    eyes ignite
             a motion all men long to wear . . .   my

                         apparition are you
             in this precarious night?   Or

        are you incarnate here?
        in this unlikely place,   in
                         this uncertain light

i dream profuse

Panther Pam, extravagant in public,
strips—fifteen pair of eyes, intense
with nonchalance, anticipate each new
exhibit of her charms and strain uneasy,
waiting for her black and velvet groin
in two/four time to rape their fantasies.
Pam facilitates imagination . . .
the lights turn green and blue and grimly white,
the darkening drummer drums the driving time,
Pam's rhythmic fingers smooth her mocha skin—
her glowing chocolate torso draws me in . . .

I feel with her, I dance I dance I must,
she flaunts with me, her haunch she swivels lust
and strokes, her nipple rising to her touch—
those practised hands obscenely promise much.

Perspiring now I know that she is more
than such a lust as mine prepares me for—
but heat and lights infuse my sweating glands
and I too dance obscene as she demands.

Flannel, my mouth my tongue too thick to cry
I ache, sweat, Sweet, I ache—deny
her sweet, my ache to suck her body dry

Contempt she laughs my fumbling heart
in blatant loving private shows her arts
and laughing smacks her lips her lewdly parts

In heave my hips by her directing hands
and dance I too as she obscene demands . . .

In dance I joy my Pam to make I scheme
and follow beat at cymbal clang I dream
profuse and caper carnal caper thrust
I steamy pour my magnifying lust
in sweat I joy says rattlesnare and drum
she visions me and fear I sometime come
to face her facing out and sheeny skin
she laughs me sweating breathing hard is sin—
I frighting does she seek my secret smell
wherewith my fetished brain in damn to dwell
me will she give me loving pleasure such
her hands her lips as promise seek me much
I want I fear in rage her massive beauty
jangle sings me husband father duty
halts her hungry breath alluring hands
I dance dance dance as drum and she demand
the snare and clang go *stop*.

                              I gape as caught
my panther dancing there is dancing not
she chesire mocks my dreaming wet and hot.

the eater, impotent

she smiled

among the others and
interrupting, neither graceless
nor gracefully, she

spoke it does not matter what
praises of my poems. And,

as she amused me,
I laughed,
observing how thoroughly she was there.

Then, speaking of what
matters now or does not
matter now, she

gave a gift,
inscribed deliberately—
"a gift for Peter Michelson."

Was it then
perhaps the gift, and
my receiving,
deliberately,

asking her name, her address
with what purpose I do not now
nor did I know, for

she was neither beautiful
nor stunning
in any way but that
she was there in such reality,
and young.

And when as of course I did I called,
she said,

                   you may bring some wine, not
              too pretentious nor yet
                        too mean, a wine, how

                   shall I say, just suitable
              for the occasion.   And,

          as I apparently amused her
     and she quite clearly me,
                   we laughed.

              Perhaps the laughter, then,
                        and the gift—giving.

              Some thing we sought
          to share.   Yes,
     yes some simple thing we hoped

                   that hovered graciously
                        to guide us through the
                   anarchies we
              breathe inexorably as air.

          She received me
     more formally,
a silken scarf brightly in her hair,
     an avocado shawl—

              as if to say,
          "respecting forms, their due,
     we may address disorders, we
                   may risk the sultry air."

          She
     brought glasses then
and cheeses on a board.

41

From grasses of my choosing she devised exotic cigarettes.

So we drank and smoked and
talked of this and that.   She

read poems to me
through the pungent air.   I spoke
it does not matter what
praises of her poems—

something perhaps
of fire, something
perhaps
of care. And

though I
do not speak of love,   there
was between us / what was penetrable / a thing we shared.

And on this bridge
I moved to her   languidly
through the conscious air.

And
as I moved to her   she moved   it
is true almost
imperceptably, yet *she moved to me.*

Each of us, then, moved.
Deliberately.   And
there followed such
doings as you may guess between
our lips and teeth
and tongues,
the

moving of her body beneath my hands.

42

And
there was between us still
the gift—

I bore her gifts
as you have guessed.
And it is true / I lusted after giving.

But,
as my lips caressed her throat, she
locked my head in her strong arms (for she

was tall and strong) and
crooned a fearful croon . . .

who are you
and who am I, and what do we desire—who are you
and who am I, and what do
you, do I desire—and

Yes, remove my clothes, she said,
beneath this candle's veiled light
that you may never leave
for having known this
auspicious night.

And yet she held me fast
and feared the fire,
crooning low and terribly
of desire . . .

Do not she said Abandon me Abandon
me Abandon me do not she said
Abandon me Abandon me Abandon me, Ah
yes, you must.
Abandon me . . .

And holding tight,
tight she crushed / from me air

and sight, she made
a trance—gripping, gripping me / as if we danced our
                                    lives' last dance:

                        and yet I felt
                    myself abandoned there   as
            if naked straddling naked air,   I
                        sought beneath her shawl and

dress I sought with
                    stroking of her skin   I
            with such manipulations reached
to touch and touching know what spectres wracked the

                        soul within her
                    supple skin.   For
            I had gifts I longed to give therein.

                    But,
                    though I held her body in my arms, and
        though my touching made her moan,   I

                        knew she was no longer there.   I
                    felt my psyche too
            like hers at large and moving freely from my will; it

                    followed her
                    in choreographies
            I could not comprehend.   And

                    though she moaned
            and writhed beneath my plunging hips

                    it was as if
            we wrestled in some baffled
                        sexless brawl, where,

                in my trance of wine and smoke and
        lust, my senses spiraled

                            44

and my thick fingers
mauled the promise
of the night. . . . still

I sought
that hot wet fabled place
of fabled
grace, and
our lunging bodies grappled

jaggedly and arched, our
only union
stress, our
bodies straining as the broken
eagle strains against the

failure of its flight,

and my distending need
buckled beneath the chaos
of my blood,

draining from my limbs and heart and
balls until

the turbine of my brain screamed
so shrill that all
my body's timbers trembling announced

the slacking
of my prick and spine and skull—

my lust collapsed, my
clot of body congealing
on the floor.

What
gifts now?   What

45

has a man to give,   a
                    mush of consciousness

                 alone,
            afloat precariously
        and groping limply for some storied shore.

        Weak and drenched
    I left her thus, yes, abandoned
                        abandoned
                    to her crucible of dreams,
            I left her thus, abandoned to her

            fitful sleep, I
    left her thus, as she had me,
                    abandoned,
            undelivered of my gifts, remembering

                the touch
        of mine upon her tongue, I left
    remembering, for still I drift and grope among the
                    rumored graces of the young.

Deserving, lady, is what I am of you and you, God knows, of me. But Deserve we dare not do—not me, not you. I know that you deserve to be, and Be is chance—and me. Deny fine caring for and knowing of desert. Dredged, denied, and hid, have me thus, aware of peril riding. And sigh when rowels rake your lovely ribs.

Come, now, like Virgil's earth unprompted, free, free with all her fruits, floods: Bidden, ride your crests to sources secret, sweet, and weak—I / we ride our dolphins diving deep. We sup and loving loving dolphin sleek, I cannot hear or see you weep, or grip you sinking ominous to sleep. And love we must and breathing deep receive exquisitely our long tormenting sea.

the garden lost

To say you
were sun to my moon, that
my shining lived
in dread of your
eclipse,
locks
my love in
antique quackeries,
metaphor.
To

say I
had a need, in you,
profound as your own deep searchings
implacably
expound, or
to say quite simply that
I love you and love
exacts unerringly
its price: to
say and know I
love and need you does
not—cannot perhaps—
now or
ever quite
suffice.   And

to say I
find now a sump where
I had before but know a
glory argues melodrama, like
tumors, in
the brain.

your garden shone so lovely
alone and rare beneath the night—
in rose and lilac bathing,
gardenias graceful, alien, and white.

You led me
from your garden
parched and praying desperately for rain.   Be-
hind I heard the subtle
bolting of the gate
exile me to
myself again.

My

love gave you
a warm unperfumed smell.   Those
smells breed dreams and dreams
I carry still.   I
had not thought
such
dreams
could sour so
soon, nor
nightmares marry me so well—

Your garden shone so lovely
alone and rare beneath the night—
in rose and lilac bathing,
gardenias graceful, alien, and white . . .

49

for kristen, in the spring of her fifth year

Monday your mother and I concluded that ("for awhile") we would no longer live together. In September, I go west alone.

Tuesday, as I watched from the window—an ominous still-life of myself—you, looking south, tossed your long auburn hair (ignited, even from that distance, by the sun) and raced into the street. A car, coming from the north, stopped at the northern edge of time.

Wednesday, before dawn, your mother and I were awakened by a tom cat groaning his heavy need. But three litters (thirteen kittens) in one year is enough. So I put on my kimono and went barefoot into the cold, wet grass. He was black, with his tail crooked sharply at the tip. I chased him off, alone, into the night. Back in bed, our feet, your mother's and mine, touched. Familiar. More affectionate than in months. Estranged. I could not get back to sleep. The cat, farther off now, continued to moan.

Wednesday evening I read you a new bedtime story, "An Elephant is not a Cat." You liked it, though before I finished you fell asleep, your chin on my shoulder where you had been looking at the pictures. But, as I put you in bed and turned out the light, you said softly, "don't close the door."   .

In September I go west. I too, alone in the dark, am afraid.

long distance
(for hilary)

Hi Daddy, you said
and, though thin and far away, *Hi* was wild   high
and happy. I

made a present for you,
for Christmas, but   I'm not going to
tell you what it is! (And
I could see your blue eyes big with delight as you shook
your long thick hair, even then on the verge
of not being able not to tell me
what it was).

Daddy, you said (all
at once precociously
rational, grown-up, and amused by the world), I

have something funny

to tell you—Jane and
me and Kristen and Kristen and me got
locked in Kristen's
room and it was two hours till her mother came home
and John and Billy had to take the door off and we
played and looked at a big book full of toys,   then
we ate dinner over./(you,

loving and warm,
thought that was funny, so
it was). Daddy,   when are you coming here?

I said about two
weeks. You said, Is that a long time?   I

said about fifteen days.
Then you counted fifteen to see how
long that was.   OOOOOOOOO-

kay Daddy—did
you get us presents?   Yes, greedy-mug,
I said.   Then you laughed and said, I

love you Daddy.
Then you blew me hugs and kisses
over the phone.

back home in indiana

(i)   indianapolis

who was being boarded in the Baniszewski
home while her parents traveled the carnival
circuit, died last Oct. 26.
a pretty lass who like the Beatles and
roller skating.
did not complain to her parents when they
made a visit in October.

burned with matches and cigarettes, whipped
with a heavy leather belt, hit on the head
with a paddle and a broom.
John Jr., now 13, and two neighbor boys,
diabetic Richard Dean ("Ricky") and Coy,
both 15.   Gertie, 39, and Paula, 18,
and Stephanie, 15.
mom burned Sylvia's fingers with a match,
she added,
it seemed like a game.
denied any part and said she was too ill.

afraid to stop the torture
released into the custody of her father,
John, who has remarried since his divorce.

afraid
too ill

Gertie started, Hobbs said, but she got
sick and told me to finish it.
testified he was courteous and accomodating.
etched tiers of inch-high block letters
across lower abdomen.
I'm a prostitute and proud of it.

three inch sewing needle.
sterilized.

courteous
accomodating

very regularly attended worship services.
my conscience bothered me all Monday
and Tuesday
Wednesday, he added, the hooked end of
a two foot anchor bolt to brand the
numeral 3.

who was granted a separate trial broke
into sobs.
quoted Sylvia,
I wish my dad was here. Just take me
home, Stephanie, take me home.
struck her on each side of the head and
told her to get up, only pretending
to be sick.

mercifully
didn't seem to be breathing anymore
gave mouth to mouth
mercifully

Sylvia's parents, still not comprehending
how and why.
Gertie, also puzzled, confided to police.
"She wanted something in life, but I
couldn't figure out
what it was."

mercifully

(did not) complain
afraid too ill
courteous
accomodating regular

conscience all Monday
and Tuesday
Wednesday the anchor
bolt mercifully
granted a separate trial
broke into sobs as
something (dad? home?) was
wanted
was
something still
not comprehending
something
didn't seem
breathing anymore was
mouth to mouth
mercifully
also puzzled was
afraid
too ill was
still not comprehending
was too ill was
looking but
was not able to
figure was it
mercy
was something fully
mercy was
mercy sobbing was
something
mercy was mercy
mercy (something) was mercy
granted
a separate trial
where they could
(not) figure it was
mercy and crying she
cried mercy and
the mercy was
she died

(ii) the crucible

for two years the
telephone a terror and
her saying oh god *I*
want you back from her trip
west her father
said her life a ruin
despicable nothing nothing give
money the house a
terror the night silent watching
empty thorazine and
sobbing halucinations of
things dying no
bullshit now but small
suicidal lies whispered
clenching her friends in the
night prayers for oblivion no
two thoughts touching de-
scend the terror of her
soft parts the slither
and sprawl of fear in the
gut all muscle and nerve and
spasm writhing belly up
to the night its silent empty
indifference probing her
nakedness her fear wrenched the
pentothal trip to terror to
a place where travellers
turn to swine and
back and back again and
the sobbing she sobbed then

the telephone the
terror I'm sorry she
sobbed gasps and convulsions her
clearest reality saying
whatever she said *I*
want you I said no I
said cry

cry
your soft parts
slithering and sprawled in
her craw gag her
father blind and despising de-
nying the night in
porcelain crystal tapestry
hate his/her terror the
night silent empty ac-
cusing he said her
nothing nothing ruins hate
and terror hate and
terror she said oh
god *I*
want whatever
she said your
hands on me your
mouth be mine pos-
sessed oh father father why
have you despised
me forgive me love
me she said whatever
she said oh my god love
me come back to me save
me *he said no* (I
carved *pity and fear*
on her naked skin her
father started to but
he got sick for
six days and nights my
conscience bothered me on
the seventh day I
placed my mouth on hers and
breathed in *no*
no no no and
the sobbing she sobbed then)
dropped the telephone to its
cradle with
one convulsive grip she

ripped the wire from the
wall her
heart lunging in its heavy
blood she
bolted the impenetrable
door to her impenetrable room and
turned stark-eyed to
the implacable
empty silent night.

(iii) south bend

"Dear Daddy,   I
have been missing you, how have you been
in Laramie?"

"I
love you very very very
very very very
                    very very very much

Daddy
Happy Valentine's Day.   Wanna

know how much I
love you?   This
much very much."

"Write me a letter please."

Then,
when we came back from
sliding Shelley's hill, me crouched in
the tobbogan, you giggling and
tight against my back,

                plowing and rolling into the
                      drifts, you held your
                boots up for me to pull them
                      off, and you

                      said, "It's
        not fun when you're not here, Daddy."

                      Later, as
                John came to take me

                to the train, you
        kissed me and said, "watch Daddy," and

                wading into the snow,
        chortling with your whole wooly body,

                      you
                fell straight back
        with your arms outstretched and
                      made an angel.   I

                have been, child, now
            as in all my quiet hours, also
                      alone,
            afraid in my parenthesis of skin.

                And you, your
            father in Laramie, Chicago, some-
                where on the circuit—your

                mother in the crucible—you
        seven years old, looking for something
        from her, from me, from home . . .
                            You too,
                            how have you been?

III

letters for the dead and the dying

airmail love lyric to olga

My love billowing, billowing, rides
beyond the Rockies—to you . . .

My song, restless, uprooted from your
calm belief, hovers stupidly about the
pain you once again, with grace, survive . . .

Your pain, the ice that seeds the cloud . . .

it brings at last your pain a warm, at
last your pain a sweet, your pain at last
a warm sweet rain.

a note, with flowers, for olga

I know
it hurts, your
old heart haranguing.   But
life, gram, has
a long elastic limit when
its roots are in the ground.   Like

this azalea—we
sent it for you to get the idea
from, just to watch the
way it does, with
the blossom bursting red on
green . . . until the petals
fall away to make
a sort of ghostly scene, maybe
making carrion for clay.   But

all the while
in that green fuse
there's the juice to
force the flower, which
comes and, coming, comes again
to seize at last its
bright-eyed hour.

for e.s.

Luxuriant before
the mirror, my
vanity preens,
draped in the rich
cloth of quiet grief you

left your kin.   Receive my winding
cloth, Remember
Death, you
might well say; but
vanity's impression now

defrays the cost
of that.   Without
the funeral pyre's flame
to char belongings, we
the living try them, find
them ours and pray the

gods our thanks, deriving
bounty from mourning's
balm.   Our molds,
yours and mine, were cut of a day,
both beneath one sign.

I wear your clothes.
I help your family pray.
Still you say, Remember
Death.   But I preen
and relish my grace-note breath.

to herschel (for helen)

My aunt died in your last winter
emaciate and wracked
with sodden years of haunted self abuse
through bootleg barbiturates and gin.
We buried her, who loved her,
and wept that she had died at last,
who at the last had only death to win.

For those whose life at last resolves in dying
there is relief, an end to grief, in crying.
But you have died without finality to things.
Your young dying is a fact I don't believe—
Two years now you're dead
and still I do not grieve
nor either does remembering relieve
my disbelieving, or bring
inspired lamentations, as I could wish to sing.

I loved you in kind
as I love now the bride you left behind,
but you leave us little
with which to feed the expectations that we need.
Unlike the ancient absent heroes,
mythic, large, and Greek,
you promise no return, provide no orchards
to confirm the confidence we seek,
nor even yet
assure us with your image
in the son you wanted to beget.

Your bride—still more bride than wife—
has been too long faithful to your bed.
That woman is made for man to fill with life,
and cannot love without the fact of flesh,

66

without some breathing on her skin,
and you, your loving parts inert,
cannot inspire her or you again.

You leave some memories, some photographs,
some personal effects.
And I have now two yarmulkes
in a drawer I open only late at night—
a black one for your burying
and for your marrying, a white.

Forgive what I presume, Herschel,
but with the luggage of your memory
I don't know what to do.
I try, I guess, to document chimeras,
to articulate some clue,
and exorcise the haunting
of the love we bore for you.

ballad of big daddy

Eugene (Big Daddy) Lipscomb was
found dead this morning in his Balti-
more apartment. The 6 foot 9 inch
300 pound professional football player
was discovered by his cousin sitting
slumped in a kitchen chair. . . . When the
cousin slapped his cheeks in an
attempt to revive him, Lipscomb
sprawled to the floor, dead. He was
still holding a hypodermic syringe with
the remains of what was apparently a
fatal overdose of heroine. Lipscomb
is not thought to have been an addict
or habitual user of the drug.

—news report

Spread-eagled
Big Daddy was collossal
in his stance; he'd coil and leap to clasp
at stars exploding white crescendoes through
a glittering angel
dance

They dance,
The angels shine and dance
and tantalize Big Daddy's desperate grasp—
but bright white angels fear so big a man,
they fear a man so big
and black

But black
men have their visions—they too

68

take their chance—Big Daddy's dream was fading
when the needle fanned it bright and now like snow
      his visions flower through
          the night

         This night
      he dissembles so and shudders
to plunge that juice, those showers, that exquisite
joy of steel releasing crimson powers—
      Now Big Daddy's dreams
         are white

        White
      dreams, now, this visionary
Caliban, this heap whose life is done
This spectre courts, at last, his own Miranda—
      This night seeker of
        the sun

Big Daddy you enter my skin exquisite, a ghost
released from my youth's ambition, and I exult
in your splintering forearm shiver and your huge
hams uncoiling the warhead of your shoulder.

Like tenderloin, I spit your body upon
my soul's erection and turn you, in a tiger's fire.
The stench alone excites my orgasm,
Big Daddy, your naked conflagration rages.

Like you, I would I could explode and let
my shrapnel spatter red the milky way—
To find me out I'd have them scrape the sky:
Abort the spheres of paradise, I say,
Let Caliban enjoy Miranda—to the hilt.

Big Daddy, Big Daddy
     sitting on a chair
Along come his cousin
     knocked him off of there

Big Daddy, Big Daddy
    sitting six feet high
Dips in the needle—
    takes him to the sky

Oh how he danced
    that night in his bed
He humped with a heave
    locomotives require

He sang, he laughed,
    and drank off his dread
Jumping with juices,
    alive with desire

Sweet Jesus . . . he's moaning,
    Big Daddy is dead.

noon, november 22
(the eater's hour is absolute)

Anguish is
this hour absolute, its
splintering crystal
glides asylum corridors,
gods
ride indifferently as hair
on Oswald's incisive
finger, my
babies bloomed
beneath your grin da
da da dada dada your
murder mocks the dreams
my babies bloomed, be-
neath, chaos.   fate.
martyrs.   murderers
fascinate our screens, this
hour is absolute its
fear splinters crystal
shatters asylum
offers martyrdom our babies, wicked
grins God's trigger
finger
curving gently
grin, I
dream with dada
God dada God grin
your killing mocks
the chaos babies bloom within

mercy is no soldier's art

"Since their induction to/the corps, these/
men have trained to/kill the enemy, and/now
in Vietnam they/have at last been/given that chance."
(Huntlybrinkly, February, 1967)

I'm here ten
months, a G.I. says, I
fought the VC plenty, but I
never saw one alive
before.   I'm on the point when I
see Charlie, he's
forty yards away, I
fire a burst then
hit the dirt right
under Charlie's guns.
He pops grenades, one I
backhand far enough it
only shatters shrapnel through
my arm, but then I see a
VC ready his grenade, I
fire, hit him in the
side, grenade it
don't go off, he
falls—a
woman, old with
stringy hair, came
crawling from a bunker to
drag away the corpse—I
hit her straight.

He saw his (long
awaited) opportunity and (straight shooter) he
hit her straight, as
he had the rifle ready she
came(stringy) crawling she came

72

(old) to tidy up or (perhaps)
retrieve her (now) dead
or someone's son and (straight
shooter) he hit her straight
not (simply) because she was
old or stringy but (why?) because
he had the rifle ready and
she (crawling) came to drag
away the corpse, a (messy) job innocuous
enough and (even) necessary though she doubtless
would have passed his ammunition on
for old (and stringy) as
she (doubtless) was she was useful to
the enemy and (herself) the second
that (straight shooter) he had
seen alive, having killed the
first and now steadying his sights to
greet the second as she came crawling to
(perhaps) commend that (now) dead soul to
Shiva or strip his ammunition or
drag his corpse away (why came
she crawling there?) and
(straight shooter) he his rifle ready
seeing his (well trained) chance he,
as she came from the bunker
crawling, he (noting with his straight
shooter's eye her hair was stringy) he
(in no position to smear his
sight with sentiment) he
hit her straight.

Now this wounded
pilot, his spattered
leg a pulp hangs flapping—
and though he's in shock he
wants the world to see (the
camera's there at his
request): as medics probe and sew I

73

gape bewitched by his soliloquy—
VC and civilians were
all mixed up we
couldn't fire I
had to hang above I got
too close and Charlie caught me I
couldn't fire and
hit civilians I
was hanging there like ducks I
couldn't fire the risk just sitting
there like ducks I
should've shot I
had the drop to
cover god damn god damn god
damn he ripped me
leg you show this back home to
Berkeley send it back to
Berkeley those punks god damn
them this is
war out here those
kids you show them this
I'd like to meet just
one god damn I
had to hang there
close too close I
couldn't fire on women Charlie
ripped me good you
let them see *I*
didn't fire VC bastard covers with
the kids and women I
ᵕtayed too long he
ripped me good *I*
want those kids to
see god damn the mucker's
beg well look goddamit
look, see this bloody leg.

The lens, that bland

exact technician, cannot
transpose your bloody leg to
wine and wafer—That
lens describes an arc of
deadly circumstance no
martyr's art or melodrama
can prevent—Oh
dismembered man, did
you think war had rules and style—like
any art's achievement mounted
for appreciation? Did
you—do we—think war the care
and feeding of prisoners to
provide the stalag
comedy for later generations? You
should know as well as Sherman and
know far more than God that
war is hell, and satan must
shoot straight and fast, blast
child, wife, or
man beyond their means to
murder you or feed the
needs of those who
will—An army marches
on someone's blood, its
belly takes any swill—
Mercy is no
soldier's art, a
soldier's only business is
to learn efficiently to kill.

for john matthias, remembering may 4, 1970

"dead as door mice, dead as door mats
dead in spite of . . .

their silliness and smiles . . ."

Susan Saxe shot a policeman. Perhaps she didn't shoot him. The newspaper said she did. Perhaps, if she shot him, she shot him because he was a pig. Maybe she thought, "policemen are pigs." So she shot him because it's all right to shoot a pig. Perhaps she shot him because she wanted a revolution. Perhaps she didn't shoot him or want a revolution. The newspaper said she did. Perhaps she didn't shoot him because she thought he was a person acting like a pig and she was confused, so she didn't shoot him. Perhaps he was a person acting like a pig. Maybe she thought the world would be a better place if she shot him. Maybe she just wanted to rob the bank (the newspaper said she shot him while she robbed a bank) and he didn't want her to rob the bank, so she shot him. Maybe he thought the world would be a better place if she didn't rob the bank.

She wrote this poem (the newspaper printed a poem and said she wrote it) and said silly things like that she didn't love her mother and that "I must have intensity." Perhaps she shot him because she was silly. Or perhaps she shot him because he was silly. Maybe she thought it was silly to be a policeman, so she shot him. Maybe he thought she was a girl and shooting him didn't seem like a thing a girl would do and she thought that was silly so she shot him. Also she said (the newspaper said) "I have no illusions that I will survive the revolution." Perhaps she thought he would shoot her and when he didn't she didn't know what to do so she shot him. He didn't survive the revolution. The revolution is for the people but lots of people won't survive it. Maybe the revolution is for somebody else. It is not for greedy people. Maybe she thought he was greedy. Maybe she thought he was greedy and mean and shooting him was all

76

right. Maybe he thought she was greedy and mean (the newspaper said she was robbing the bank) but wasn't sure whether it was all right to shoot her so she shot him instead.

John has a new baby daughter, Laura. She is greedy and mean. Her mother's nipples are very sore and her mother is very tired because Laura won't sleep at night and cries instead. Laura doesn't care about her mother's nipples or how tired she is. John's other daughter is two. She is also mean and greedy. Also she is silly. I have two daughters. They are greedy and mean and silly. So am I. So is John. Greedy . . . Mean . . . Silly . . .

IV

pacific plainsong

preface to *the works* of h. h. bancroft

volume XXXI (history of washington, idaho, and montana,
1845-1889)
pp. vi and vii

There were those determined to
serve not (as Vancouver) by
stepping on shore to luncheon and
reciting (ceremonies) to the
winds, nor by naming the
great River of the West for
(as Robert Gray had done)
his ship. There
were those who
served (as they determined) by
possessing there were those determined
servers determined (while securing to
themselves such homes as they might
choose) who by possessing
(of the territory) chose
to serve by taking there
were those who (by possession) chose
securely there such homes as
those (determined) who declining
luncheon and some ceremonies, chose
to serve and did (their
government) by taking territory
and (ceremonies to the winds) they
served by actual occupation.

I need not here repeat their
narrative I need not here
repeat those (bold) measures by
which these men of destiny their
destiny achieved. I
wish only to declare they

faced (those early pioneers) the
mystery, they faced the
great unknown—though (by whimsy, by
merest chance, or as we say
it fell out that) they
had found the choicest portions—
they had (of the great unknown)
found its fertile soil, its
wonderful inland sea, safe
from storms, always open to navigation,
abounding in fish, bordered
many miles wide with
the most magnificent forests on earth.

So (securing to themselves such
homes as they might choose) it
did (does) not require
a poet's vision to picture
a glowing future, albeit dim
in the reaches of time. And
to lay ever so humbly destiny's
corner-stone was worth the (humble)
toil and privation (abounding
in fish) the (safe from storms)
danger and the isolation (always
open to navigation) for
to lay destiny's corner-stone
(even) ever so humbly is worth it and
there were (weren't there)
among them those determined to serve.

Yes, and (incidentally)
this inland sea with
treasures inexhaustible of
food for the world and
fifteen hundred miles of shore covered
with pine forests to the
water's edge and

surrounding it small valleys of
the richest soils, watered
by streams from pure
snows of the Cascade
and Coast ranges, half prairie and half
forest, warm sheltered from winds enticing
the weary pilgrim from the eastern side
of the continent to rest in
their calm solitudes, so well did
God (and those who were determined to) serve

(though it was true that
the native wild man
still inhabited these valleys and
roamed the mountains to the number of
thirty thousand, the
incomers were sons of sires who
had met and
subdued the savage tribes of
America as they
pushed West from Plymouth Rock
to the Missouri and beyond—
therefore they had now no hesitation).

For bred to believe
that British and Indians would
melt before them they
(British and Indians melting before them)
had no hesitation and
(though there were among them
native wild men) they
(sons of savage sires) had
no hesitation and (bred to believe
in melting pots) they melted
British and Indians before
them and (determined
to serve) enticed weary pilgrims
to their calm solitudes for

83

there were (calm, determined) those
men of destiny facing
the great unknown there
were those bold those
determined who (securing to themselves
such as they might) chose
not (unrequired) a poet's
imagination (the British and Indians
melting) for among them were
the sons of sires determined
to serve and they (securing what
they chose) they had (picturing
a glowing future) they had therefore
(without ceremony) they had therefore now no hesitation.

The sources for this volume are those which have enabled me
to write all my volumes.

"though coming to them under color of peace, it was charged upon the chief that he intended to entrap them. however this may have been,

the volunteers, not content with
putting so powerful an enemy out of
the way, amused themselves that evening in camp by
cutting off bits of his scalp as
trophies; and when the scalp was
entirely gone, the assistant surgeon of
the regiment cut
off his ears,
and it was said some
of his fingers . . .
Parrish probably exaggerates
when he says: They
skinned him from head to
foot, and made razor-straps of
his skin."
He (Parrish) probably
exaggerates. For it's unlikely that
the head, hands, or feet could be skinned
efficiently, the best incision (easiest) being to
cut from the neck base splaying
down the spine bypassing the rectum (arcing right
and left) across smooth buttock blubber to
the scrotum (keeping the tool flaccid and ground
ward, the indians so far as we
know being the first American sister and mother
fuckers), continue the seam down the inside of each
thigh to the ankle, encircling incisions around
ankles, privates, arms (usually not
worth their hide, excepting extraordinary
biceps) and neck, then simply peel
hide from carcass (being careful
about the ribs) and stretch to cure—though I

should note that of all skins
the human is suited more for ornamental
than productive purposes, and will not
strop a razor well, so he (Parrish) probably
exaggerates. The volunteers (perhaps) amused
themselves with bits of scalp and ears and
(it was said) some fingers, but most certainly
he (Parrish) goes too far in saying they
made razor-straps of skin. And
though the volunteers were enter-
prising men they (after all) were
men and Waiilatpu in December is
not (even today) an amusing place and
as the Walla Walla girls weren't (it may be
supposed) putting out to the enemy
the Oregon yankees (resourcefully)
amused themselves in camp, though
it would exaggerate to say they (like
Shriners) went too far and surely he (Horace
Greely) exaggerates (like Parrish) to
say (in 1858), "The enterprising territories of Oregon
and Washington have handed into congress their
little bill for scalping Indians and violating
squaws" for (as history records) truth must beware
exaggeration and most certainly they
bleed too much who say those
volunteers excessively amused
themselves in camp with
bits of scalp and ears and (it was
said) some fingers

"Thus perished the wealthy and powerful chief of the Walla Wallas."

on the beach at lapush

Locked in locked
in this (neither past nor
present) anachronistic village is
shrouded in its battered sea
spray air—its shoreline stacked
with stoney bleached enormous (two
feet thicker than
a man is tall) carcasses
of trees, their jagged roots upended
claw the (sullen) sky—all
all is shroud and bonewhite gleaming
along this brittle shore

A (well past bearing) squaw
rocks amid the baskets she
no longer weaves and looks beyond the mist
bound shore complaining men no longer ride
the open boats or
risk rough water out at sea.
In the village (white) Mark
Westby teaches indians (one or two) their
ancient craft of carving—offshore
Shell Oil blasts leviathan
and salmon, sounding lively
messages of profit through this pall
of spray. But I came to see
fishers at their trade, and
their past a curio,
their present obsolete

I watch the ghosts of Kwakiutl,
oil skinned and glistening, astride
the pitch and swell, they
work their dark pacific

87

sea and bend to haul up gleaming
nets, to bring rich flesh
of fish to air; their
calloused fingers slap the
gaff deep in the heaving
gills they snare—implacably
they gaff that signal writhing,
gaff
and know an old despair.

leschi, scene treatment for a many humored musicale

(From Telstar) camera pans
whole of continental U.S., at
Seattle zooming to
intersection of Yesler Street (original skid
road) with Elliot Bay waterfront to
(chief) Leschi, then, wearing Brando/Zapata
expression of (profound)
ennui and dedication, standing at
corner—fish trucks, tourists, and
stevedores in background, as
Mac and Muff (teeny boppers) play
(discrete) grabass, watching jellyfish
orgasm in the bay. All is
tranquil and godfearing
bustle of enterprise when
Leschi (in war paint, headress, and bear's
tooth necklace) shakes
a tambourine and bellows, "White Mother
fuckers," then (having just the night
before seen Sammy Davis Jr. as a t.v. cavalry
sergeant) adds, "Black Mother
fuckers!" All freeze agape (except Mac in slight
grimace as Muff, freezing, catches his
foreplay digit in sphincter
lock), Leschi begins war
dance, chanting Nisqually
medicine ("The times they are
achangin," punctuated at
grace notes with lyrical *White*
and/or *Black Muahfu*) and
prancing about intersection plunging
a harpoon through tires and
denting hoods and fenders with
tomahawk. All freeze until traffic cop comes

89

to and shouts "All right, Mac, Cut it!"
(Mac, misunderstanding, looks up
terrified, frantically doubling
efforts at digitus
interruptus from rigid Muff), Leschi
ignoring cop continues his demonic
attack on Yesler and waterfront. The cop
unable to solicit help, as
all hold freeze, launches into "Indian
Love Call" which awakens Muff (much
to Mac's relief), who is
in real life a beautiful octoroon Nisqually
princess studying voice at Cornish
School and she (loving men in
uniform) responds with Kundry's seduction
aria from "Parisifal" which
baffles cop until they get together in
duet of "God Bless America (and nobody
else.)" They exit (after encores) to
an emergency cop phone and call
the riot squad which
comes and pounds Leschi (who continues throughout
chanting and prancing oddly about banging,
poking with tomahawk and harpoon until
subdued) to Burgerchef tenderized consistency, as
camera pans from business-as-usual at
Yesler and waterfront while the traffic cop is
locked with Muff in an inarresting sex
arrangement, as (close up)
jellyfish undulate in bay.

Scene two opens in courtroom, as
prosecutor concludes, ". . . from every
lamppost, by the good Lord above we'll
have law and order in this
land." The jury goes
berserk, foreman grabs up a flag, others
produce fife and drum, all march and sing "Yankee

Doodle" around the courtroom. Spectators remain
calm though fuddled. As Public Defender
shrieks, "My client, even though a filthy, backward
savage, pleads not guilty, but
personally I wasn't at the scene of
the crime so
it's hard for me to say."
Jury starts up again but judge
gestures hypnotically with
outstretched palm. "What," he asks
Leschi, "have *you* to say?"
Leschi gestures hynotically (gives
judge the finger) and shouts *White Mother*
fucker; sees a black cop, *Black Mother*
fucker! Cop keeps stoneyphizz but
straightens smart black leather
cravat and adjusts smart black leather
ammo holster belt, resting
hand on revolver butt, eyes
smiling *Man it more blessed*
to give (shit) than receive (it)—
every motherfucker for himself
(sings "Ol' Man River").
Public Defender interjects to
(bug-eyed, outraged) judge
"My client means this
whole thing is mistaken, he's
just an actor studying his
role on the street, but
personally I wasn't at the scene of
the crime so
it's hard for me to say."

Pandemonium again, until
Prosecutor cries, "Objection, his
act's too good, Yesler Street's no
stage for pissant players to
buggar traffic while

91

they hone their mocking
methods . . . We're witness here
to muckrakery and (reason)
treason spreading *seeds* throughout the land. I
call on witnesses to (lie)
testify: this bad good actor's stopped
up traffic . . . *He whomped my hood, Dented
my truck, Was up to no
good, Why he said fuck!* Too
much! The judge leaps up shrieking, "If
niggers can by God learn not to
shit in corridors and keep
a tight zipper on their fly (Black
cop covertly checks his) then
you stinking savages can learn to
live like Christians (jury
cheers, spectators, still calm and
fuddled, applaud) and (by God) you're GUILTY
GUILTY GUILTY and we'll (by
God) make you all good (dead)
injuns or know the (by God) reason
why" (Jury foreman leads "locomotive"
for Law and Order) as
(from Telstar) camera pans whole
of continental U.S. and
orchestra overlays muted "America
the Beautiful" on electronic reverberations of
Everett Dirkson reciting (in
unctuo) *with liberty and justice for all* . . . as
Leschi goes to gallows

and " . . . on the 19th of
February the unhappy
savage,
ill and emaciated
from long confinement and
weary of a life which
for nearly three years had been

92

one
of strife
and misery, was
strangled
according to law."
strangled according to law
the law according to
which he strangled
was law
(according to law)
and he was strangled
according to perhaps not his
law
but according to some (which?)
law
he was strangled and
according(ly)
he
dangled
from and jerked about (dares
Justice jerk her lovers off
the) gallows (?) That
act's tough to follow, but
before "a large concourse of people (there) assembled"
he (weary) according(ly)
according to some
perhaps not his
law he
(an emaciated method
actor studying the lead
for his own life
story) was
strangled
according was
strangled according to law.

Though few chiefs survived it and
"His (Leschi's) death may be said to

have been the closing act of
the war on Puget Sound,"
"Kissass (stet) Kussass, chief
of the Cowlitz, (lived)
114 years. He
was friendly, and a Catholic."

waiilatpu

Knowing depravity from Calvin
old Marc Whitman must have
died smiling, as a
jagged Cayuse hatchet jellied
his relentless brain . . . One
hundred years prove
he didn't smile
in vain. This happy
valley reeks with God's
inexorable plan, his
grace: here
Whitman came with
Calvin's god and small
pox malignantly in
hand; with Augustin's heart
burnt cork he smeared
alien stone
age souls, he
dipped their well
pocked bodies in this
valley's many waters—at
Walla Walla vestigial un-
elected savages atoned
grim souled Swiss or
rare Babylonian
sins.

Waiilatpu, place of
rye grass, once
ground for this
valley's native councils,
now it honors
Whitman, his
mission and his

kin. His hilltop
monument tapers to the
sky—a finger gesturing
abuse, enshrined, officiously
fenced in. Down
the hill, across
a road, beyond
the mission's old
foundations, a rutted creek
bed commends the
Walla Walla and
Cayuse, drained long
since and dead.

seattle is described as a dignified and venerable per-
sonage, whose carriage reminded the western men of
senator benton; but I doubt if the missouri senator would
have recognized himself . . . in this naked savage who
conversed only in signs and grunts.

Sealth, your brazen
image labors now beneath the
bowels of pigeons, or
now and then a gull will
bring you tidbits from the
bay. Your moulded eyeballs gaze
on produce of the land you've
vanished from—at this post card skid
road square, at tourists, sailors, cops, sullen
indians, and reeking Yesler
bums. Chief, my (suburban) youth was fed on
myths of your (pacific)
wisdom. Our ancestors loved you (we were
told) and named their town for
you. You weren't (like Kitsap) pushy or
(like Leschi) mad. You knew
your place. And (footnotes to your history say) you
taxed the settlers (shrewdly) for these restless
nights you walk, your ghost
unearthed by (chatty) invocations of
your name. That fraud vindicates a
savage (naked) born and remnant to
the Age of Reason. You
learned the game. History footnotes (at least) a man
who bites a dog or an injun who
screws a white man without
contracting clap. Counsellor, even
though (poor bastard) you didn't have the
style of a (Missouri) senator, you
counselled well to keep your tribe from

war. The Dwamish fished
in peace, were dry and warm in
winter, and died a quiet
death. They
extinguished themselves with dignity. Knowing
your (civic) duty, you merchandised
your cosmos to these states. So
now I come to see your (memorial)
reward, to Yesler where your noble profile
sits, your
brazen headress gleaming
in the rain, and
your stern (prophetic) glare ignores
the shoulder (twitching) where
a balding eagle shits.

Nor mountain no
nor bronze nor
stone are monument
gargantuan howevermuch
enough

Though Crazy
Horse
emerge at last from South
Dakota hills, his
mountain blasted tombstone's
pork barrel boondoggle
DRAG
show, (See Folks, step up, look close—
beneath the Breechclout,
stone)

A concrete buffalo three
storeys high gazes
down a North
Dakota draw, hot
for cows that never
come

98

gargantuan howevermuch
enough.

Air ripper, jack
hammer, blast, beam, and
balls we shape
Mohammed in the mountain, lament and
scan the edge of earth: such
remembering—poem, plate, or
song—is molding
making all horizons take
cadavered shape.

Emerge at last though
Crazy Horse he
may from South Dakota hills his
ghost is
friendly.
(Him good injun)

Custer died for your sins
says redskin   bumper wit.
But vestigial Sitting Bull, amused,
knows more precisely who wins,
how little the sea churns
or earth burns to pay for sins.
When Joseph, who survived White Bird Canyon,
Big Hole and Absaroka,
survived the treachery of Assiniboines and Crow,
was hounded thirteen hundred miles by Sherman's Army,
haunted by starvation, cold, spectres of extinction,
When Joseph sent to Sitting Bull for help
he (the Custer killer) said
Joe, do you, like Crazy Horse, expect some miracle from these hills?
You might as well piss upstream
to keep water from the dam—
give up, man,
Custer was a bad scene from a (B) flick—
but the ultimate (comedian) is Uncle Sam.

No matter how the sea churns
or earth burns to pay for sins
the guy that lasts is the one who wins.

In 1866 old Seattle watched
the sun, at Alki, extinguish, ripple orange, warm and
conjure sachems, their shimmer, his eyes, visions,
shimmer trails behind the sun—Seattle, tired
and prophetic in his impotence, saw old ghosts (no
ghosts) ghosts in '66. He learned
from Jesuits, and mad Leschi's execution, to
read graffitti on statehouse (outhouse) walls.

Nor mountain no
nor bronze nor
stone are monument
gargantuan howevermuch
enough

Seattle, this naked savage who conversed in signs and grunts,
says to President Polk:
Day and night cannot live together. The red man has ever run
before the white man, as morning mist before the morning sun.
But your proposition seems fair. My people will accept the
reservation. We will live apart in peace. The words of the
white chief are the words of nature speaking to my people, speak-
ing out of a dense darkness. . . .
It matters little where we pass the remnant of our days—they
will not be many. A few more moons, a few more winters . . .
tribe follows tribe, and nation nation like the waves of the sea—
that is nature's order. Regret is useless. Your decay may be
distant, but it will surely come. Even the white man whose God
walked and talked with him as friend with friend cannot deny
his destiny. We may be brothers after all. We shall see. . . .

(this land is ours

or yours your ships your
cavalry confirm
the stars are sky is
dark our visions dark our
gods gone your
god grins your
cavalry your ships confirm
his grin it
matters little where
we pass our days your
guns diminish gods your grinning
cavalry confirms
it little matters I
shall not mourn I
shall forget my
god I
shall sign your deed this
land is my tribe is
blood this land is graves holy
ashes holy land is mine is
sacred ours
or yours
your cavalry your gods and dead
leave their land or graves wander
fields beyond the sun our
dead remain their dust is
rich with blood white
man the dead are bloody
dust white
man the dead are dust
dust prevails our
dust we bathe
bloody our visions white
man you will never be
alone be just
remember blood the
dust is not without its power.)

In the morning fog off Alki in the bay
Decatur's cannon prowls.
Dolphins arc before her dripping prow,
and from the sky
gulls crash clams against
the indifferent shore's rewarding stone.

Nor mountain no
nor bronze nor
all the elegies of man are
monument gargantuan howevermuch
enough

dakotah plainsong

Now there is no heron here,
starkly poised,
its spur uplifted
from its shadow, subtle
on the darkening stream—
No kinetic fisher waits
vertical and still
to strike, eat, stretch,
and swing above the hills—
The hills, their autumn lines,
their opulence at dusk,
deceive serenely
and belie this leaving plain
which wears
like sixty years of suet
wear away the teeth
and leave blunt stumps
in withered gums—
Weather marks
these plains,
scattering their signs
of enterprise—
the hogan of the Mandan,
the tipi of the Sioux
are splintered
through the badlands'
withering display—
For weather marks
these plains
and men
root this futile
dirt, they
grow

sweet briar
and strawberry wire
and sour wine,
while the winter heron hurries
to lily, germander, and columbine.

"bestride the mighty and heretofore deemed endless missouri"

an essay on the corps of discovery

i

On the eastern slope
some were brazen, bold
as brass—the
young squaws even occasionally
hustling a ride in the strange up-river
sailing ship (a curious custom with the Sioux
and as well the Pawnee, they
give handsome squaws to those whom they wish to
show some acknowledgement. The
Sioux we got clear of
without taking their squaws.
They followed us two days.
They persist in their civilities. . . .)

But once past the Divide things were different. The Shoshone
women who had no word for white man but *tab-ba-bone*, enemy,
were as if prophetically afraid. Coming within 30 paces un-
expectedly of three female savages, they appeared much alarmed
but saw we were too near for them to escape by flight. They
therefore seated themselves on the ground holding down their
heads as if reconciled to die.

Sun-burnt, Lewis looked to be her natural enemy, but
when he stripped his shirt, showing
his white belly she appeared, he said,
instantly reconciled.
For the instant, as he took the old woman
by the hand and raised her up
gave her beads, moccasin awls, pewter mirrors and
painted her cheeks with vermillion, which
with this nation is a sign of peace, she

was no doubt for the instant,
as he said, reconciled. Now more than ever,
though she appeared otherwise to Lewis and
perhaps herself, she
was reconciled to die.

Her men, though armed and expecting enemies, the
Minnetarees, were disarmed by these pale apparitions
bearing gifts. Embracing
fate affectionately, in their way, they
place the left arm on our right shoulder
clasping our back while
they apply their left cheek to ours, saying
ah-hi-e, ah-hi-e.
I am much pleased.
I am much rejoiced.

Then the ceremony of the pipe
the sacred pledge of friendship, barefoot,
vulnerable and exposed, honoring
three times from East to North the points of the heavens—
the stem to the earth
then to the white men
then one another. Making
as only the women seemed to know
their peace with death. . . . "Several of the old
women were crying and imploring the Great Spirit
to protect their warriors, as if they
were going to inevitable destruction."

The Corps of Discovery came in peace.
They came with blue beads.
And scarlet red vermillion.

On the western slope of the Bitteroots, as they approached the
first Nez Perce village, most of the women fled to the neighbor-
ing woods with their children, a circumstance he had not ex-
pected as Captain Clark had previously been with them and

informed them of our pacific intentions. The men seemed but
little concerned and several came out to meet them, unarmed.

Later, as if some aboriginal players devised the scene, Broken
Arm took flour from the roots of cows and thickened the soup
in the kettles of all his people, inviting those who would abide
by the council to come and eat and those who would not should
abstain. All but one, an old man, celebrate the feast.

And outside the lodge
the women, he said, cried, wrung their hands, and
tore their hair. The women, he noted,
filled the air with lamentations. The women
with their heads bowed to receive death.
The women riding with their children to the hills.
The women
always the women
filling the air with lamentation. What,
in their fear, in their womanly weakness, in
their women's hearts, what did they know
that he, Lewis, meticulously
noted their fear and lamentation?

He told the chief, Cameahwait, he was sorry for their lack of
trust. He told the chief that among white men it was considered
disgraceful to lie, to entrap an enemy by falsehood . . .

(there were yet he hoped some Shoshone
not afraid to die. Or have you all, he said,
the hearts of women, and noted
again meticulously
that he had "touched the right string."
No, the chief said, I am not afraid to die.
The solemnity of the pipe, then.
And the women imploring the Great Spirit
as if, he noted, they were going
to inevitable destruction . . .

107

Exultingly he thanked his God that he had lived to bestride the
mighty and heretofore deemed endless Missouri.

ii

York
the big black buck
"servant" Clark said
the way a Virginia gentleman don't say *slave* or *nigger*
don't say *shit* if he had a mouthful.

Said, "canoes of skins passed down from the two villages and
many came to view us all day, much astonished at my black
servant who did not lose the *opportunity* [my italics] of display-
ing his powers, strength &c. This nation never saw a black man
before."

May be—can't say—they
never either saw a "servant" before.
Better they get used to it.
Going to see it a lot.
Going to be it. Soon enough
going to be more big
bad black curly haired bozos in Dakota
than Pawnees.

Those aborigines much astonished at my servant indeed!
York carrying on with his powers and all,
not missing the opportunity. *He*
ain't getting no medals, large *or* small size,
picture of Jefferson. . . . All
flocked around and examined him
from his nappy burr head to his two-toned
pink and black toes. *He* don't miss
no tricks. . . . carried on the joke, he said,
and made himself more terrible
than we wished him to do. Yeah,

108

old York coming down *bad* right there at the start.
Don't miss a trick, putting them
Pawnees on. A little show,
black boy doing honest-to-god *black face*
right there on the prairie—heart of America.
Just, God knows, a little bit
badder than we wished. But OK
a little divertisement
in the middle of the big play.

Break out the fiddle now,
show them shuck footed Pawnees some *rhythm.*
He ordered his black servant
to dance, which (naturally)
amused the crowd
much, and even somewhat astonished them
that so large a man should be active &c.
Those people are much pleased with my black servant.
And he don't miss a trick,
showing off his powers. . .

(and their women, fond of caressing . . .)
old York must of had himself a time, their
women very fond of caressing
caressing I dare say
his powers, and
his powers getting bigger by the minute
making himself more terrible than
we wished and
you can make book on it too.
Old Step 'n' fetchit
being *baaad* right out there beyond the frontier,
just laffin and showing off his powers . . .

    (there once was a Pawnee maid
    who said she wasn't afraid
    to lay on her back
    in a prairie shack

and let a *black* cowboy !?
diddle in her crack.
And then to her surprise
her belly began to rise . . .)

Ohhh   Yassuh, Yassuh the dancer said
and then for prophecy
he ate her.   Marsa Clahk, he
winks and says, you think *that's* fun,
you just waits til later.

What history records is that he made himself more terrible than
we wished.

iii

    Courageous, resourceful, and enterprising they had, Jefferson
knew, "the true qualifications."   Though lacking "a perfect knowl-
edge" of botany, natural history, morality, mineralogy, and
astronomy, they were in the end therefore found to be more
reliable, American.   More importantly, they were soldiers, men
of skill and discretion in the use of arms—muskets of startling
accuracy, the swivel gun, menacing, solid, authority unequiv-
ocally in its sweeping range.

    And, though imperfect, they were men of their time, sci-
entific—observant, pragmatic, detached . . . enabling them to
record flora, fauna, topography and native customs without preju-
dice (those people, Clark noted, are dirty, kind, poor, and ex-
travagant, possessing national pride, not beggarly, receive what
is given with great pleasure, live in warm houses, large, octag-
onal, forming a cone at the top left open for the smoke to pass,
covered with earth on poles—willows and grass prevent the
earth passing through.   Those people express an inclination to
be at peace with all nations.

    Meanwhile, we tried the prisoner Newman last night by nine

of his peers. They "did sentence him 75 lashes and disbanded from the party." The punishment of this day alarmed the chief very much. He cried aloud, or affected to cry. I explained the cause of the punishment and the necessity for it. He also thought examples were necessary, and he himself had made them by death. His nation never whipped even their children, from their birth.

(Note: the Arikaras are not fond of spiritous liquors, nor do they appear to be fond of recieving any or thankful for it. They say we are not friends or we would not give them what makes them fools. Those people express an inclination to be at peace with all nations.)

Also, they were practical and canny in matters of defense, enabling them to succeed where others failed—knowing only too well that *the treachery of the aborigines of America and the too great confidence of our countrymen in their sincerity and friendship has caused the destruction of many hundreds of us.* Those people express an inclination to be at peace with all nations.

Then too they were men exemplary not only in their skills but also in their morals, inspiring loyalty and discipline in the field. On Christmas eve a Clatsop chief offered a woman to each of them, which they declined accepting of, and displeased the whole party very much, the female part, especially. This was the same party which had communicated the venereal to several of our party in November last. I therefore gave the men a particular charge with respect to them, which they promised me to observe. Old Dlashelwilt and his women still remain, but I believe, notwithstanding every effort of their winning graces, the men have preserved their constancy to the vow of celibacy which they made on this occasion to Captain Clark and myself.

No wonder, then, that they should fulfill their president's charge—to ascend the Missouri to its source, to cross the Highlands, to locate and follow the best waterway from thence to the Pacific Ocean, to establish friendly contact with the aborigines, to assert thereupon the power of the White Father over their trade, comfort, and well being, to make vocabularies of native languages, to make maps, chart geography, collect horticultural, botanical, zoological, and anthropological specimens, and "as indeed they did" make way for a prosperous commerce.

Courageous, resourceful, and enterprising, they knew, meticulously and instinctively, how to touch the right strings. Though lacking a perfect knowledge, they were in the end found therefore to be more reliable, American. The fruit of America. American. Those people always expressed an inclination to be at peace with all nations.

iv

From the beginning they
were received with curiosity, and
nothing more whetted interest in their mission than
an exhibit of musketry and cannon. Which
they did regularly and with great effect. Always
of course advising that
the new White Father in Washington, he
who had bought them from the anarchists
of France, he who had bought them from the
monarchists of Spain, he
the White Father
who brought them the Word, he
desired to live and trade in peace with the aborigines.
And he, they said with what sense of irony we
do not know, he desired that
they live with one another so.

(*Look back, they told Little Crow, the
Mandan war chief, with
what sense of irony we do not know, look
back at the number of nations who have been destroyed by war.
Reflect, they said, on what you are about to do.*

If he wished the happiness of his nation he
would be at peace with all.   By
that, by being at peace, and
having plenty of goods, and a free intercourse with
those defenseless nations, they
would get, on easy terms, a
greater number of horses . . . if
he went to war, he
would displease his Great Father, and
would not receive that protection and care, as
other nations who listened to his word.
Happiness, horses, easy terms, *they said.*
Listen to his word.)

Among the Mandan they thought it well to aid and assist them against their enemies, particularly those who came in opposition to their councils. If the Sioux were coming to attack, to collect the warriors and meet them. The chief said the village was very thankful for the fatherly protection, that the village had been crying all the night and day for the death of the brave young man who fell, but now they would wipe away their tears and cry no more.

Rejoice, they said.
Listen to his word.

Among the Wallawallas several diseased persons requesting medical aid, to all of which we administered, much to the gratification of those poor wretches. We gave them eye-water. *It would, Clark said, render them more essential service than any other article we had it in our power to bestow.* A little before sunset the Chymnappos joined the Wallawallas and formed a half circle around our camp, where they waited very patiently to see our party dance. The fiddle was played and the men amused themselves with dancing about an hour. They were much pleased at the dancing of our men. I ordered my black servant to dance, which amused the crowd very much, and somewhat astonished them that so large a man should be active &c.

113

They then requested the Indians to dance, which they very cheerfully complied with. They continued until ten at night. Accordingly took leave of these friendly, honest people.

Among the Nez Perce, a reception more equivocal. Here too we dispensed eye wash and liniment, gaining for our medicine, as Clark said, an exalted opinion (in our present situation, I think it pardonable to continue this deception. . . . *We take care to give them no article which can possibly injure them.*)

At dinner however
an Indian fellow very impertinently threw
a poor, half starved puppy nearly
into my plate by way of
derision for our eating dogs, and
laughed very heartily at his impertinence. I
was so provoked at his insolence that
I caught the puppy and threw it
with great violence at him and
struck him in the breast and face, seized
my tomahawk and
showed him by signs, if he repeated his insolence
I would tomahawk him . . .

> *(thereafter, he—Lewis—notes*
> *the suggestions of an old man who*
> *observed to the natives that*
> *he thought we were bad men and*
> *had come, most probably,*
> *in order to kill them . . .*

So, as all the principal chiefs were present, they thought it advisable to enter more minutely into the views of our government, its plans for the natives of this western continent, its intention of establishing trading houses for their relief, its wish to restore peace and harmony, above all the strength, power, and wealth of our nation, their well being at the disposal of its will, &c. Then, they amused themselves with demonstrating the power of magnetism, the spyglass, compass, watch, air gun, and

sundry other articles equally novel and incomprehensible to the
savages.

(still, in his journal, the
record of what the old man thought and said,
that we were bad men and had come, most
probably, in order to kill . . .

After we had eaten a few roots, we spoke to them and gave
each a medal of the small size with the likeness of Mr. Jefferson,
and to some the sowing medals struck in the presidency of Wash-
ington. We explained to them the design and importance of
medals in the estimation of whites, and as well the red men who
had been taught their value.

(still, in his journal, the old man . . .

The Nez Perce held a council on the morning of the 18th.
They resolved to listen to his word.
Then Broken Arm, the chief, took
flour from the roots of cows and
thickened the soup in the kettles of all his people.
He made a harangue, impressing
the need for unanimity . . . .
Happiness, horses, and easy terms.
They listened to his word.

Meanwhile he—Lewis—scrupulously
reported, outside the lodge the women
cried, wrung their hands, and tore their hair, as
if, he said, they
were going to inevitable destruction.
And the old man
the old man said we were bad men, bad
men who had come, most
probably, to kill . . . . *And the women, he*
recorded, cried
and tore, he said, their hair.

Having himself lived to watch
McNeal straddle the creek and
thank his God that he had lived to
bestride the mighty and heretofore deemed   endless
Missouri, he–Lewis–noted, the
evening of August 18, that
he had this day completed his thirty-first
year. (He
> spent the day in commerce, bartering a uniform
> coat, a pair of leggings, a few handkerchiefs,
> three knives and some other small things "the
> whole of which did not cost more than about $20
> in the United States" for three "very good
> horses" from the Shoshone.)
Having, though he did not know it,
completed about half of his expedition and
nearly all of his life, he
conceived that he had "in
all human probability now existed
about half the period which I am to
remain in this sublunary world." As
always, in consciousness and style, he
was a man of his age and did not, like McNeal,
thank his God but spoke grandly of
sublunary contrition. He
reflected that he had as yet done
but little, very little, to
further the happiness of the human race, or
to advance the information of
succeeding generations. But,
as yet a man of his rotarian age, he
dismissed that gloomy past and
resolved in future to redouble his exertions
and at least endeavor to promote those two
primary objects of human existence–to
live *for mankind*, as
he had heretofore lived *for himself*.

A man of his age.
On occasion grand and grandly spoken.
On occasion gloomy and alone,
pacing, while others sailed, the shore.
Alone of that resourceful, courageous, and
enterprising band, the
fruit of destiny's own breed,
Lewis alone of those
recorded the women and the old man.
Lewis, the moody, the solitary,
perhaps four years later the suicide.
An old Nez Perce man, he said,
who thought they were bad men and
had come, most probably, in order to kill.
And the women, who cried
and wrung, he said, their hands and
tore, he said, their hair.
Lewis alone recorded the women and the old man.

Lewis, who made the savages sensible
of their dependence on the will of our government for
every species of merchandise as
well for their defense and comfort.
Lewis, who took care to give the children
of the White Father no article which
could possibly injure them. Lewis
who dispensed medals of large and small size.
Lewis, who with his medicine, his weapons, his
audacity, his ambition, his genius incarnated
the spirit and power of his country . . . this
same Lewis remarks the old man's prophecy and
that the women wailed.
Did he reflect, for all
that he advanced the information of succeeding
generations, did he reflect on his
resolve to live for mankind, did he, four
years later at Grinder's Stand on the Natchez
Trace, did he, reflecting, know

as he morosely squeezed the trigger
finger of his always disciplined hand, did
he know, remembering his trek through the savage
sublunary world, did he know,
remembering the women and the old man, did he,
at the fulcrum of past and future,
scanning as a haunted man dark horizons in
that dark night, did he
see and seeing know, whoever
triggered his long night dying, did he
know precisely, having traveled to its far edge
and back, did he know, as
he cut his biography in half, did
he know precisely why and what he, reliable
American that he was, had done?

The Corps of Discovery came in peace
bearing the word, blue beads,
and scarlet red vermillion.

vi

For that we were no scholars
and lacking a perfect knowledge we
were found to be more reliable, American.
We followed absolute as mortal man can do
our high command. And
we came, as the old man said,
crudely calculating probabilities, as
the old man said and Lewis strangely noted,
we, the fathers of our sons, the
sons of our fathers, were
bad men and we came, most probably, to kill.

For coming without knowledge of what we did
we were bad men. For
pacifying the Nez Perce with eye-wash, liniment, and

laudenum we were bad men.
For thinking we came in peace we
were bad men. For bringing Virginia manners
to the Nez Perce we were bad men.
For our courage we were bad men.
For our strength we were bad men.
For failing to know the probability of our being
bad men we were bad men. For
bringing the badness of men to our fellow man
in the service of our country
we were bad men. We
were bad men, as the old man said, bad
men who came, *knowing well that the treachery*
of the aborigines of America and
the too great confidence of our
countrymen in their sincerity and friendship has
caused the destruction of many hundreds of us, and
we came, by any historical calculation, we
came most probably, whatever we supposed, we
came, as our leader's journal remains
to remind us, we came most probably in
order and well prepared to kill.

Accordingly, we took our leave
of these friendly, honest people.